PAPER CRAFTS FOR VALENTINE'S DAY

Randel McGee

Enslow Elementary

an imprint of

Enslow Publishers, Inc.

40 Industrial Road
Box 398
Berkeley Heights, NJ 07922
USA

http://www.enslow.com

Dedicated to all the valentine girls in my life:
Marsha, my wife; Mable, my mother; Melanie, my daughter;
and Emma and Lily, my granddaughters.

I want to especially acknowledge the late Duke Kraus, puppeteer and humorist,
who came up with the idea for pop-up puppets; a sample of one is in this book.
Duke showed the idea to Rob D'Arc, puppeteer, showman, mentor, and friend,
who improved the design and then showed them to me.

This book meets the National Standards for Arts Education Standards.

Enslow Elementary, an imprint of Enslow Publishers, Inc.
Enslow Elementary® is a registered trademark of Enslow Publishers, Inc.

Library of Congress Cataloging-in-Publication Data

McGee, Randel.
   Paper crafts for Valentine's Day / Randel McGee.
      p. cm. — (Paper craft fun for holidays)
   Includes bibliographical references and index.
   Summary: "Explains the significance of Valentine's Day and how to make Valentine's Day-themed crafts
      out of paper"—Provided by publisher.
   ISBN-13: 978-0-7660-2948-4
   ISBN-10: 0-7660-2948-4
   1. Valentine decorations—Juvenile literature. 2. Paper work—Juvenile literature. I. Title.
   TT900.V34M34 2008
   745.594'1618—dc22   2007014041

Printed in the United States of America

10 9 8 7 6 5 4 3 2 1

To Our Readers: We have done our best to make sure all Internet Addresses in this book were active and appropriate when we went to press. However, the author and the publisher have no control over and assume no liability for the material available on those Internet sites or on other Web sites they may link to. Any comments or suggestions can be sent by e-mail to comments@enslow.com or to the address on the back cover.

Every effort has been made to locate all copyright holders of material used in this book. If any errors or omissions have occurred, corrections will be made in future editions of this book.

♻ Enslow Publishers, Inc., is committed to printing our books on recycled paper. The paper in every book contains 10% to 30% post-consumer waste (PCW). The cover board on the outside of each book contains 100% PCW. Our goal is to do our part to help young people and the environment too!

Illustration Credits: Crafts prepared by Randel McGee; Photography by Nicole diMella/Enslow Publishers, Inc.; Shutterstock, p. 5; Courtesy of Brian Enslow, p. 25.

Cover Illustration: Crafts prepared by Randel McGee; Photography by Nicole diMella/Enslow Publishers, Inc.

CONTENTS

VALENTINE'S DAY!

Many years ago, Emperor Claudius II of Rome wanted to create an army of soldiers that cared only about serving him. However, his married soldiers cared more about their wives and families than about their emperor. The emperor made it against the law for young people to get married. A Christian priest named Valentine saw how unfair this law was. Going against the emperor's orders, Valentine secretly married young couples in love. When the emperor found out, he had Valentine thrown in prison. Valentine became close friends with the jailer and his daughter. February 14 was the day he was going to die for disobeying the emperor. On the way to his death, Valentine plucked a flower for the jailer's daughter and sent it to her with a little note that said: "From your Valentine."

When Christianity grew, the church leaders declared February 14 as a holiday to remember Valentine and his caring deeds. The old Roman Lupercalia traditions continued with boys and girls choosing partners for the day. All this is what lead to celebrating Valentine's Day as a day of friendship and love.

Be My Valentine!

The celebration of Valentine's Day spread throughout France during the thousand years after Valentine's death. The first known Valentine's Day love letter was written in 1415 by a Frenchman named Charles, duke of Orleans. He wrote the letter to his wife while he was a prisoner in the Tower of London. By the 1600s, Valentine's Day became a popular holiday in England. In old England, children would dress up as adults on Valentine's Day and parade around their neighborhoods.

In the 1700s, the English and French began sending small gifts and handwritten letters of affection to loved ones and friends. The English colonies of the United States, Canada, and Australia also joined in the celebrations of the day. In the middle 1800s, printed valentine cards became a popular way to send love and greetings on this day. Get ready for Valentine's Day with the cards, decorations, party favors, and gifts described in this book. These crafts are sure to please those special people in your life.

CUPID FIGURE

Cupid was the god of love in ancient Roman mythology. He was born with the wings of a dove on his back and started flying around almost at birth. In the myths, Cupid flew around with a bow and arrows dipped in a strong love potion. The invisible arrows were to make people fall in love, sometimes when they least expected it. Cupid is a popular symbol for Valentine's Day. Here is a hanging version of Cupid that you can make.

WHAT YOU WILL NEED

- ✎ tracing paper
- ✎ pencil
- ✎ white card stock
- ✎ markers or crayons
- ✎ scissors
- ✎ white glue
- ✎ clear tape
- ✎ ruler
- ✎ string

WHAT TO DO

1. Use tracing paper and a pencil to transfer the pattern on page 39 to the card stock.

2. Decorate and color the figure with the markers or crayons as you wish. Cut out the pattern.

3. Fold the figure along the lines shown.

4. Glue the extensions of the wings to the back of the cupid figure. Glue the hands together. Let dry.

5. Use two small pieces of clear tape to fasten a 14-inch piece of string to the back of the figure.

6. Ask an adult to help you hang the figure from the ceiling or a window frame.

HEART SCULPTURE

The valentine heart is one of the most popular symbols on valentine cards and decorations. It is a symbol of love and devotion. In ancient times, the heart was thought to be the center of strong feelings, like love. How the red, round humps that taper to a point became the symbol for the heart and love is not really known, because it does not look a lot like an actual human heart. However, it is a popular symbol on Valentine's Day and is used in all types of decorations. You can create a decorative sculpture with this project.

WHAT YOU WILL NEED

- ✎ tracing paper
- ✎ pencil
- ✎ poster board of any color
- ✎ scissors
- ✎ markers or crayons
- ✎ clear tape
- ✎ cotton balls
- ✎ white glue

WHAT TO DO

1. You will be making six hearts. Use tracing paper and a pencil to transfer the patterns from page 40 to the poster board. Cut out the patterns. Cut the slits as marked on the patterns. Decorate the hearts with markers or crayons.

A)

2. Connect four hearts by sliding them together along the slits. Two hearts will be upside down and two will be right side up (See A). Use clear tape to hold the hearts in place. Make a square with the hearts and tape the ends together (See B).

B)

C)

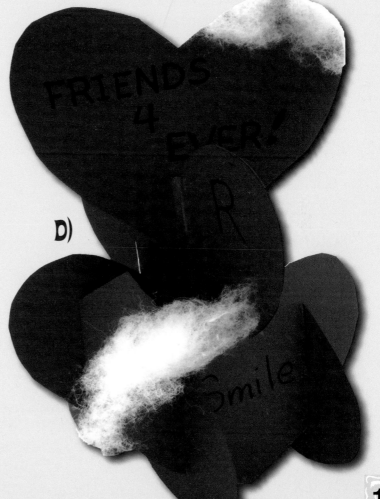

3. Connect two hearts by sliding the slits together (See C). Attach these two hearts to the heart square.

4. Pull off pieces of cotton balls to look like fluffy clouds. Glue them as you wish to decorate the sculpture (See D).

D)

Lacy Heart Card

In 1847, in the United States, young Esther Howland, the daughter of an American printer, received a beautiful valentine card from England decorated with lace. She made some valentine cards of her own to sell. She used bits of paper lace, ribbons, and colored paper. They were very popular! Soon she had to hire her friends to help her keep up with the demand for her cards. Now, nearly one billion valentine cards are exchanged every year in the United States, Canada, Mexico, the United Kingdom, France, and Australia. Here is a paper lace valentine card that you can give.

What you will need

- white office paper
- red office paper or construction paper
- scissors
- hole punch (optional)
- white glue
- markers or crayons

WHAT TO DO

1. Put a sheet of white paper and a sheet of red paper together. Fold the papers in half. Cut a half-heart shape. (See page 41 for the pattern.) Unfold. You now have two paper hearts.

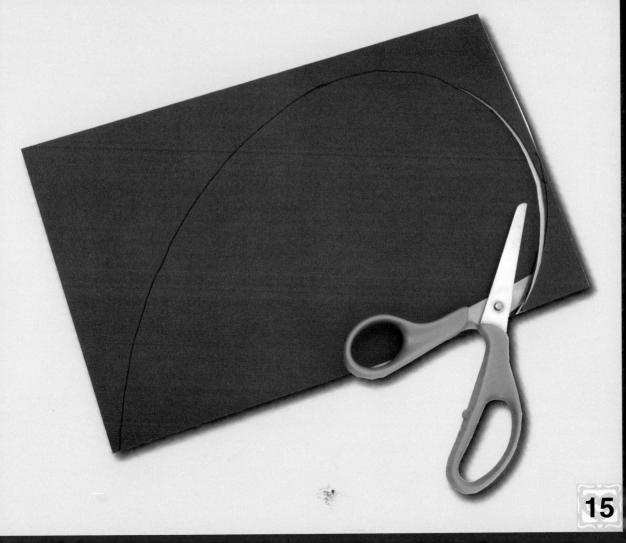

A)

B)

2. Fold the white heart in half lengthwise (See A). Cut designs along the edge. Cut small hearts, flowers, or other shapes in the paper (See B). Use a hole punch to create designs if you wish.

16

3. Glue the white heart to the red heart. Let dry.

4. Use markers or crayons to write your special valentine message.

POP-UP HEART CARD

No one knows for sure who put the first paper pop-up figure in a greeting card. People started to put moving paper parts into books during the 1300s. In the 1800s, printers added moving paper designs to greeting cards that could change pictures or make raised shapes. Today, there are even organizations devoted to the art of moving paper designs or "pop-ups." Here is a simple yet fun way to make a pop-up valentine card.

WHAT YOU WILL NEED

- ✎ white and red card stock
- ✎ scissors
- ✎ white glue
- ✎ markers or crayons
- ✎ construction paper, any color

WHAT TO DO

1. Fold the white card stock and red card stock in half widthwise, so that the short sides meet.

2. Cut a large heart from the red card stock. (See page 41 for the pattern.) Lay the red heart in front of you and fold the outside edges in to meet in the center.

3. Open the folded white card stock and match up the center lines of the red heart and the white card. Glue the folded edges of the heart to the white card. Let dry.

4. Lift gently on the center line of the red heart while carefully closing the white card. Decorate the front of the card. Let dry.

5. Decorate the inside of the card with markers or crayons. Let dry. Write your message.

VALENTINE HEART CROWN

Are you having a Valentine's Day party? Be the king or queen of hearts for your party with this fun and simple paper crown. You could even make crowns for your party guests!

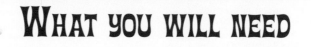

WHAT YOU WILL NEED

- ✎ poster board in any color, 8 inches x 14 inches
- ✎ tracing paper
- ✎ pencil
- ✎ scissors
- ✎ markers or crayons

- ✎ white glue (optional)
- ✎ glitter (optional)
- ✎ glitter glue (optional)
- ✎ sequins (optional)
- ✎ stickers (optional)

WHAT TO DO

1. Fold the poster board in half widthwise. Use tracing paper and a pencil to transfer the pattern from page 42 to the poster board. Cut out the pattern. Cut along the solid lines.

2. Decorate the crown with markers, crayons, glitter, glitter glue, sequins, or stickers. Let dry.

3. Push the smaller heart in and pinch the fold. To wear the crown, gently bring the hearts forward and place on your head.

HEART FLOWERS

Flowers have always been given as a token of love and affection. They are very popular gifts to give on this day of romance and love. Valentine's Day is the busiest day of the year for florists, the people that sell flowers. Roses are the most popular flowers to give for the day. More than 180 million rose blooms are sold for this holiday alone in North America. Here are some roses made with real "heart" to share with your favorite valentines.

WHAT YOU WILL NEED

- ✎ tracing paper
- ✎ pencil
- ✎ construction or office paper in any color
- ✎ scissors
- ✎ white glue
- ✎ drinking straw
- ✎ green crepe paper
- ✎ clear tape

WHAT TO DO

1. Use tracing paper and a pencil to transfer the petal patterns to colored construction or office paper. (See page 43 for patterns.) Make five large heart petals, four medium ones, and four small ones. Cut out all the pieces.

2. Cut out a small circle of construction or office paper. (See page 43 for the pattern.)

A)

3. Glue five large petals around the paper circle. Glue the medium petals around the circle on top of the large petals. Glue the small petals around the circle on top of the medium petals (See A). Let dry.

B)

4. For the stem, wrap the drinking straw with the green crepe paper (See B). Tape the ends.

5. Cut two or three leaf shapes from the green crepe paper. (See page 43 for pattern.) Glue or tape the leaves to the stem (See C). Slightly fold all the petals up. Tape the flower to the stem.

C)

5. If you wish, make more heart flowers for a beautiful bouquet.

Valentine Heart Pop-Up Puppet

Do you have a hard time sharing your feelings? Here is a funny little valentine puppet that can help you say what you want. This puppet has a very simple move to make his mouth open and shut and his head pop up and down. You will need to help your puppet find its voice. Puppets are a lot of fun.

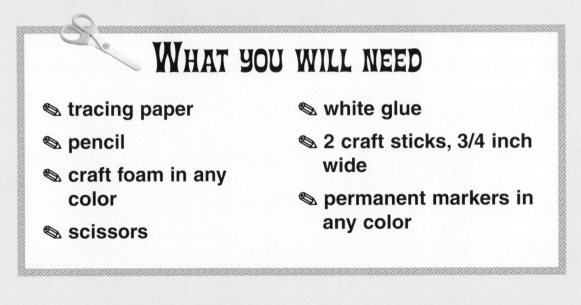

What you will need

- tracing paper
- pencil
- craft foam in any color
- scissors
- white glue
- 2 craft sticks, 3/4 inch wide
- permanent markers in any color

WHAT TO DO

1. Use tracing paper and a pencil to transfer the puppet patterns from page 38 to the craft foam. Cut them out.

2. Glue the square of craft foam to the top of one of the craft sticks. Let dry. Use a dark permanent marker to color the craft stick from the bottom of the foam square down to about the middle of the stick (See A). Let dry.

A)

3. Set the other craft stick on top of the first craft stick lengthwise. Glue one end of the foam strip to the top craft stick in the middle of the stick. Wrap the strip around both sticks and glue the loose end (See B). Let dry.

4. Glue the head pattern to the foam square on the first stick. Let dry. Glue the body pattern over the strip in the middle. Glue the chin pattern to the top of the second stick (See C). Let dry.

C)

5. Decorate the puppet with permanent markers and other pieces of craft foam as you wish. Let dry.

6. Make the puppet's mouth move by holding it in your fist and sliding the first stick up and down with your thumb (See D.).

D)

Danish Woven Heart Basket

This heart-shaped basket is actually a Danish Christmas ornament. Families in Denmark would decorate their Christmas trees with handmade paper ornaments. This woven heart works well for Valentine's Day, too! It can hold a special note, little gift, or candies for your valentine. It is a bit trickier to make than most other crafts in this book. Once you make your first basket, try with different colored or patterned papers.

What you will need

- ✎ **red and white office paper**
- ✎ **tracing paper**
- ✎ **pencil**
- ✎ **scissors**
- ✎ **ribbon, in any color, about 10 inches long**
- ✎ **ruler**
- ✎ **white glue**

WHAT TO DO

1. Fold one red and one white sheet of office paper in half widthwise (See A).

2. Use tracing paper and a pencil to transfer the pattern on page 41 to the folded papers. Be sure to place the edge of the pattern along the folded edge of the paper. Cut them out (See B).

A)

B)

3. Cut along all the solid lines (See C). Each pattern now has three strips. Place the red and white paper pieces at a right angle (90 degrees) to one another.

C)

4. Put the first white strip through the first red strip. The second red strip then goes through the first white strip. The first white strip then goes through the third red strip.

D)

5. The second white strip goes around the first red strip. (The first red strip should go through the second white strip.) The white strip goes through the second red strip. The white strip goes around the third red strip. (The red strip should go through the white strip.)

6. The third white strip is woven like the strip in step 4 (See D). The two papers should now make a little heart-shaped basket. It may take some practice and patience to get it just right. Keep trying!

7. Glue a 10-inch long ribbon to the inside of the basket on both sides of the top to make a handle or hanger (See E). Let dry.

E)

PATTERNS

Use tracing paper to copy the patterns on these pages.
Ask an adult to help you cut and trace the shapes.

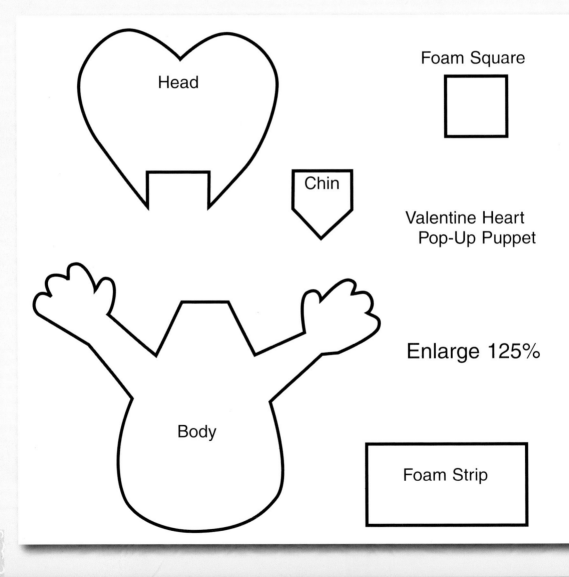

Head

Foam Square

Chin

Valentine Heart
Pop-Up Puppet

Enlarge 125%

Body

Foam Strip

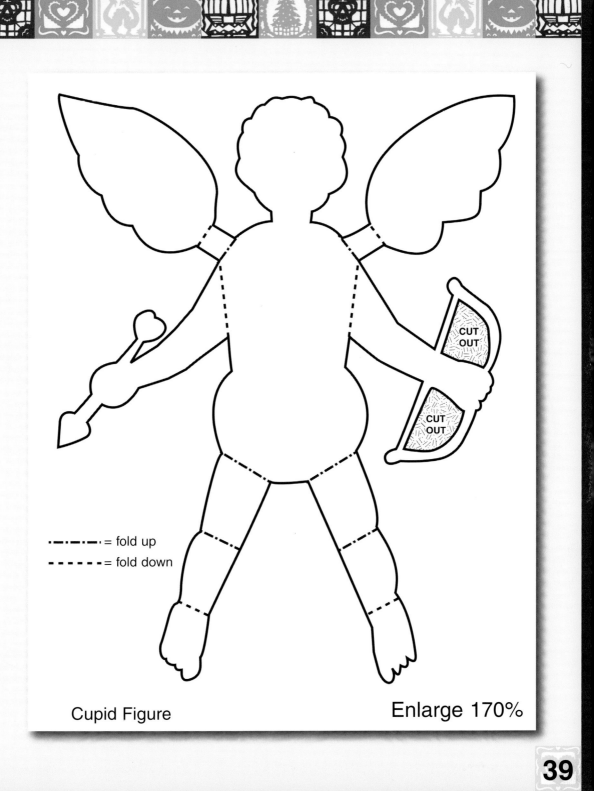

= fold up

= fold down

CUT OUT

CUT OUT

Cupid Figure

Enlarge 170%

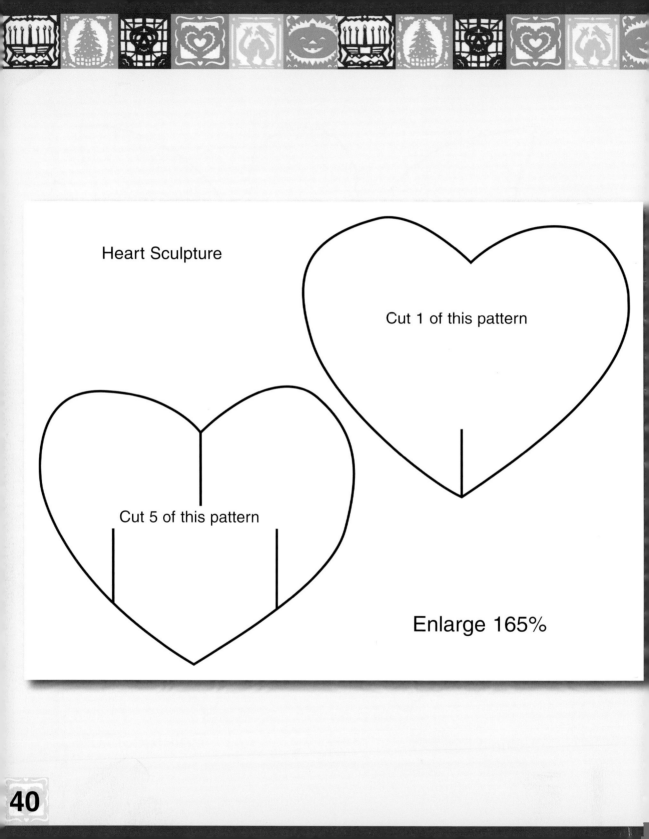

Heart Sculpture

Cut 1 of this pattern

Cut 5 of this pattern

Enlarge 165%

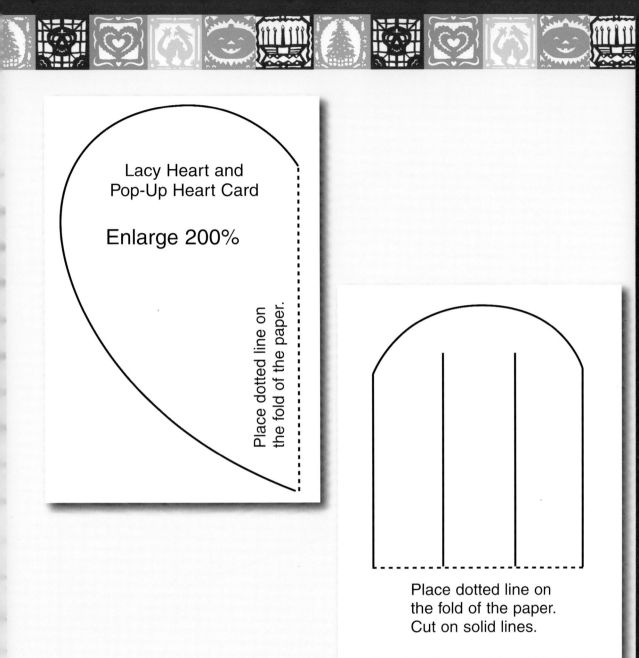

Lacy Heart and
Pop-Up Heart Card

Enlarge 200%

Place dotted line on
the fold of the paper.

Place dotted line on
the fold of the paper.
Cut on solid lines.

Danish Woven Heart Basket
(Cut 2—one red and one white)

Enlarge 200%

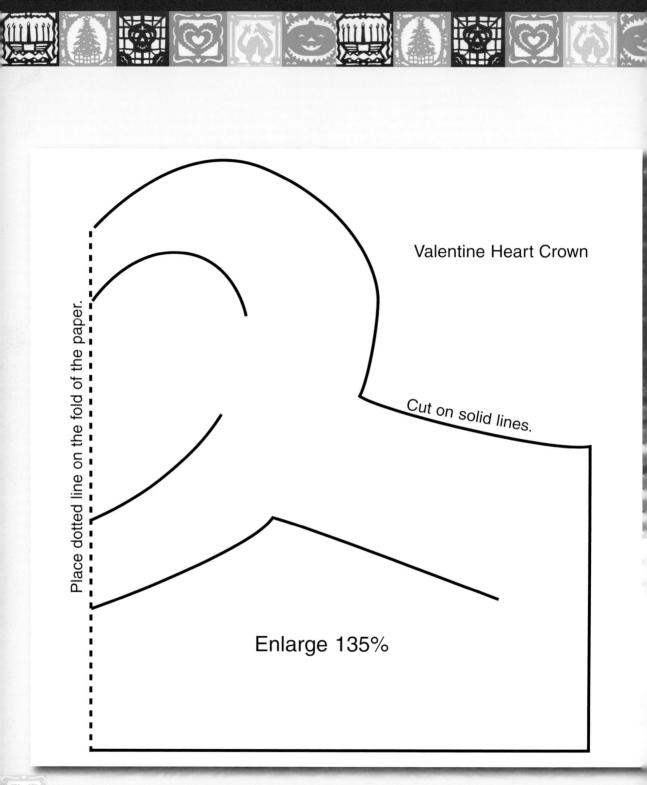

Valentine Heart Crown

Cut on solid lines.

Place dotted line on the fold of the paper.

Enlarge 135%

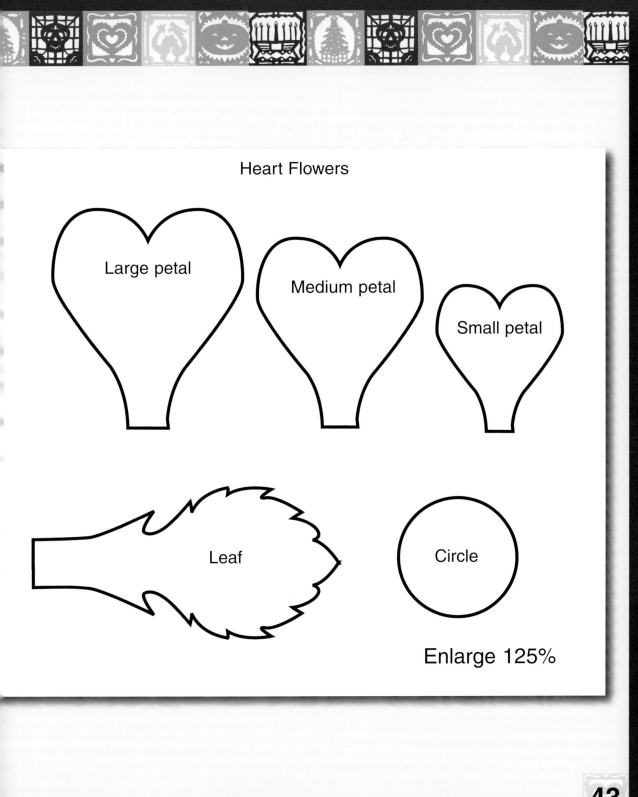

Heart Flowers

Large petal

Medium petal

Small petal

Leaf

Circle

Enlarge 125%

43

READ ABOUT

BOOKS

Gibbons, Gail. *Valentine's Day Is . . . .* New York: Holiday House, 2006.

Hopkins, Lee Bennett. *Valentine Hearts: Holiday Poetry.* New York: HarperCollins Publishers, 2005.

Rosinsky, Natalie M. *Valentine's Day.* Minneapolis, Minn.: Compass Point Books, 2003.

Tompert, Ann. *Saint Valentine.* Honesdale, Penn.: Boyds Mills Press, 2004.

INTERNET ADDRESSES

Celebrate! Holidays in the U.S.A.: St. Valentine's Day
<http://www.usemb.se/Holidays/celebrate/
  valentins.html>

The History of Valentine's Day
<http://www.history.com/
  minisites/valentine/>

Visit Randel McGee's Web site at
<http://www.mcgeeproductions.com>

INDEX

About the Author

Randel McGee has been playing with paper and scissors for as long as he can remember. As soon as he was able to get a library card, he would go to the library and find the books that showed paper crafts, check them out, take them home, and try almost every craft in the book. He still checks out books on paper crafts at the library, but he also buys books to add to his own library and researches paper-craft sites on the Internet.

McGee says, "I begin by making copies of simple crafts or designs I see in books. Once I get the idea of how something is made, I begin to make changes to make the designs more personal. After a lot of trial and error, I find ways to do something new and different that is all my own. That's when the fun begins!"

McGee also liked singing and acting from a young age. He graduated college with a degree in children's theater and specialized in puppetry. After college, he taught himself ventriloquism and started performing at libraries and schools with a friendly dragon puppet named Groark. "Randel McGee and Groark" have toured throughout the United States and Asia, sharing their fun shows with young and old alike.

Groark is the star of two award-winning video series for elementary school students on character education: *Getting Along with Groark* and *The Six Pillars of Character*.

In the 1990s, McGee combined his love of making things with paper with his love of telling stories. He tells stories while making pictures cut from  paper to illustrate the tales he tells. The famous author Hans Christian Andersen also made cut-paper pictures when he told stories. McGee portrays Andersen in storytelling performances around the world.

Besides performing and making things, McGee, with the help of his wife, Marsha, likes showing librarians, teachers, fellow artists, and children the fun and educational experiences they can have with paper crafts, storytelling, drama, and puppetry. Randel McGee has belonged to the Guild of American Papercutters, the National Storytelling Network, and the International Ventriloquists' Association. He has been a regional director for the Puppeteers of America, Inc., and past president of UNIMA-USA, an international puppetry organization. He has been active in working with children and scouts in his community and church for many years. He and his wife live in California. They are the parents of five grown children who are all talented artists and performers.